For Sarah Ward

'*I looked, and behold a pale horse: and his name that sat on him was Death, and Hell followed with him.*' (Revelation: *6, 8*)

Pale Horse was first performed at the Royal Court Theatre Upstairs, London, on 12 October 1995. The cast was as follows:

Charles	Ray Winstone
Lucy	Kacey Ainsworth
Undertaker	Terence Beesley
Vicar	Howard Ward
GP	Lynne Verrall
Maître d'	Howard Ward
Woman in Cemetery	Lynne Verrall
Woman Drinker	Lynne Verrall
Drinker One	Terence Beesley
Drinker Two	Howard Ward
Police Constable	Terence Beesley
Woman Police Constable	Lynne Verrall

Directed by Ian Rickson
Designed by Kandis Cook
Lighting by Johanna Town
Sound by Paul Arditti

The action takes place over a period of about four weeks at various locations around south London.

PALE HORSE

Joe Penhall

The Royal Court Writers Series published by
Methuen Drama in association with
the Royal Court Theatre

Royal Court Writers Series

Pale Horse was first published in Great Britain in the
Royal Court Writers Series in 1995
by Methuen Drama
an imprint of Reed International Books Ltd
Michelin House, 81 Fulham Road, London SW3 6RB
and Auckland, Melbourne, Singapore and Toronto
in association with the Royal Court Theatre
Sloane Square, London SW1N 8AS.

ISBN 0 413 70410 6

A CIP catalogue record for this book is available from the British
Library

Typeset by Wilmaset Ltd, Birkenhead, Wirral
Printed in Great Britain by Intype, London

Act One

Scene One

Bar.

Charles *is speaking on a wall phone and holding an unopened bottle of rum.*

Charles   I know. I know. I know. I know.

Pause.

I didn't know that.

Pause.

I didn't know that either.

Pause.

Because I believe in giving people a chance.

Pause.

No. I sacked him.

Pause.

Because he was a wanker. The point is I've now got six cases of Navy rum on my doorstep and no staff.

Pause.

Six bottles I asked for.

Pause.

Captain Morgan.

Pause.

I'm not selling it on – it's not a chain letter.

Pause.

Who's going to buy six cases of Navy rum? It's evil-looking.

Pause.

She's OK. The very oxygen I breathe.

Pause.

No, she can't stand the place. Thinks it's a 'den of iniquity'.

Pause.

How can it be a den of iniquity? Nobody comes here.

Pause.

I gotta go. Ta ta. Yeah, ta ta.

He hangs up and it rings immediately. He lifts the receiver and hangs up. It rings again. He answers.

Hello.

Pause.

That's me.

Pause.

What about her?

Pause.

When? Where? No, I didn't know ...

Pause.

I'll come down.

He hangs up and stares straight ahead.

Scene Two

Funeral Parlour.

Charles *and an* **Undertaker** *stand either side of a body in a bag on a slab.*

Charles   You've done a good job.

Slight pause.

It's very lifelike.

Undertaker   I haven't done it yet.

Charles   Oh.

Pause.

Undertaker   I've done the preliminaries but embalming is a laborious, very specialised process.

Charles   Why's that?

Undertaker   Eh?

Charles   What makes it so specialised?

Slight pause.

Undertaker   I don't discuss the embalming process with relatives.

Charles   No, go on. What happens first?

Undertaker   I can't discuss it.

Charles   I'm curious. I might find it . . . therapeutic.

Undertaker   I drain all the blood out and I replace it with formaldehyde to preserve the flesh. I suck the blood out with this piece of apparatus here and pump in the embalming fluid with this one here.

He holds up a piece of apparatus.

The blood goes in a big white bucket and when I've finished it goes down the drain.

Charles   You can't reuse it? For a transfusion or something?

Undertaker   Can't reuse it, more's the pity.

Charles   Not even if she left herself to science?

Slight pause.   The **Undertaker** *checks a clipboard.*

Undertaker   How do you mean?

Charles   Would you have to save it?

Undertaker   Did she or didn't she?

Charles   No. But hypothetically, if that happened, would you have to hang on to the blood?

Undertaker   They keep it at the hospital.

Charles   Oh.

The **Undertaker** *looks at him.*

Pause.

Charles   I'm making conversation. At times like this it's recommended you make conversation.

Slight pause.

Because it's science, isn't it? And science isn't ... emotional.

Slight pause.

It's unemotional.

Slight pause.

Like the weather. What's the worse job you've ever done?

Undertaker   I don't talk about that stuff.

Charles   No, you're all right, I'm interested.

Pause.

Undertaker   Suicides.

Charles   Suicides, really?

Undertaker   Found a young woman last week by the tracks at Southfields. Head completely severed. Body remained undiscovered for weeks. Picked her up, entrails gushed out in a puddle at my feet.

Charles   No.

Undertaker   Little children larking about, bringing their dogs along. I ask myself, Why? Week in, week out, dealing with the mutilated and the rotted and the dead. It's very sad.

Pause.

You want to know which type of people kill themselves the most?

Charles   Which?

Undertaker   People with families.

Charles   Right.

Undertaker   And people without families. Lonely people. Single people.

Charles   Single people?

Undertaker   Sometimes one goes and another follows. Sometimes it's like dominoes and the whole lot go. It's what life does to us. It kills us.

Silence.

Charles   Any money in it?

Undertaker   You reap what you sow.

Silence.

Any thoughts on a coffin?

Charles   I don't want anything flash. Bit skint at the moment.

Undertaker   Well there's a nice teak just come in that's a bit special. Brass handles, silk lining and a kind of domed top with an arched support. It's nice.

Charles *gazes at the corpse.*

Undertaker   It's very discreet. I'll show you a catalogue. When do you fancy the funeral?

Slight pause.

Mr Strong?

Charles   As soon as possible. A weekday.

Undertaker   Weekdays are booked out until the weekend I'm afraid. Less traffic on the roads. I could do a Monday, only not this Monday.

Charles   Whenever.

Undertaker   I can do a weekend only, again, you've left it a bit late for this weekend.

Charles   Just do what you have to do.

He gently reaches into the bag and strokes the face of the corpse.

Could I say goodbye?

Undertaker   Be my guest.

Charles *leans down to kiss the corpse.*

Undertaker   Hey, don't kiss it.

Charles   Why not?

Undertaker   It's unhygienic. More than my job's worth.

Charles   Oh ... sorry.

The **Undertaker** *goes.*

Scene Three

Cemetery.

A **Vicar** *and* **Charles** *stand by a grave. The* **Vicar** *scatters dust into the grave.*

Vicar   ... Then shalt the dust return to the earth as it was: and the spirit shall return unto God who gave it. Amen. Now let us turn our attention to Charles, to whom I give this counsel in his loss: 'Have ye not read in the Book of Moses, how in the bush God spake unto him, saying I am the God of Abraham, and the God of Isaac, and the God of Jacob?

Slight pause.

He is not the God of the dead, but the God of the living.'

Charles   No. I haven't read that.

Slight pause.

So. What now?

Vicar   The grave is filled in and you go home.

Charles   I meant, what should I do now?

Vicar   You don't do anything. The gravediggers do all that.

Charles   Should I say some more prayers or something?

Vicar   Would you like to?

Charles   Which ones?

Vicar   Any ones you like.

Charles   I don't know any.

Vicar   Perhaps you have a prayer of your own.

Charles   Make one up, you mean?

Vicar   Yes.

Charles   Something about her. Personal.

Vicar   Absolutely.

Charles   About, you know, how lovely she was, stuff like that?

Vicar   'Whatsoever things are true, whatsoever things are just, whatsoever things are pure, whatsoever things are lovely ... if there be any virtue, if there be any praise, think on these things.' Philippians, chapter four, verse eight.

Charles   Right.

Vicar   Have you read the Bible?

Charles   No, as it happens. Never had cause to.

Vicar   Was it not read to you as a child?

Charles   Family of agnostics.

Vicar   Ah. 'The appropriate title of Agnostic.'

Charles   Well, it's just C of E for atheist, innit?

Pause.

My grandad was a God-fearing man but my mother said she let go the hand of the Lord during the war. Because of the rationing and the evacuations. She didn't see a banana until she was eleven.

Slight pause.

Said it was 'taking the piss'.

Slight pause.

Sorry.

Vicar 'I gave my heart to know wisdom and to know madness and folly: I perceived that this also is vexation of spirit. For in much wisdom is much grief: and he that increaseth knowledge increaseth sorrow.'

Charles What does that mean?

Vicar You are of a generation which searched for self knowledge and identity through science. And it's no surprise when something happens, a fundamental sorrow alights, you find it perplexing.

Charles So what do I do?

Vicar Everybody deals with the passing on of a loved one differently.

Charles On average, what do they do? Any little titbits will do.

Vicar I can't advise you.

Charles No, but you could –

Vicar I listen. Such is the dilemma of faith that there is no advice, only the words of the scriptures. I am not an 'intermediary'. If you wish to petition the Lord, with supplication, you do so directly. You pray.

Charles So you just –

Vicar I listen.

Charles You –

Vicar I listen and perhaps guide you in –

Charles Well why don't you then?

Pause.

Vicar   Perhaps you'd like to come to a congregation. Share your grief.

Charles   Share my grief?

Vicar   Yes.

Charles   Share it with who?

Vicar   The community. Have you not heard 'how good and how pleasant it is for brethren to dwell together in unity'?

Charles   I keep myself to myself.

Vicar   Only the bretheren we deserve are manifest.

Charles   How d'you mean?

Vicar   I mean, the people we come to love in this life are only the people we deserve to love.

Charles   'The brethren we deserve are manifest?'

Vicar   Thieves, for example, are thick as thieves because the only people they know are thieves.

Slight pause.

Charles   I like that. Well put, Father ...

Vicar   Reverend ...

Charles   Eh?

Vicar   You just converted me. Or promoted me.

Charles   How d'you mean?

Vicar   In an Anglican parish you don't have priests. I'm a vicar.

Charles   Oh.

Pause.

It's quite complicated, innit.

Pause.

D'you think she might be up there watching me?

Vicar   Of course.

Charles   D'you think she's smiling?

Vicar   Yes.

Charles   I bet everybody smiles in the kingdom of Heaven, don't you think, Reverend?

Vicar   Perhaps you'd like something to read.

He hands **Charles** *his Bible.*

Charles   I'll have a bash. Thanks.

The **Vicar** *goes,* **Charles** *examines the Bible.*

Scene Four

Doctor's.

Charles *sits opposite a* **GP** *who makes notes when appropriate.*

Charles   ... Bus drivers ... I find myself losing my temper with perfectly normal bus drivers and it's not just because of what happened.

Pause.

Always stopping too late or stopping too early, slamming the brakes on, they drive like they got a club-foot some of them. It just makes me want to hit somebody.

GP   I do understand, Mr Strong.

Charles   They're so careless.

GP   But we all have these trials to contend with. We'd all love to lash out and get things off our chest but we live in a society governed by rules and it's these rules which are holding it together.

Charles   It's doing my head in.

GP   Personally, there's people I'd love to hit. Then I think to myself, 'I'm a doctor ... My God!' You see?

Pause.

Has anything else been troubling you?

Charles   I'm having nightmares. I dream of finding my mother and father lying murdered in a pool of blood, or I get shot, or the till gets robbed, my car gets stolen . . . I mean, what next?

GP   It's all part of the grieving process. Your mind is probably very restless at the moment.

Charles   You think they're telling me something?

GP   I'm not a psychiatrist.

Charles   Have a stab.

GP   It's more than my job's worth to attempt the work of a specialist.

Pause.

Charles   I've had other dreams. I dream about sex all the time.

GP   Yes.

Charles   Sex with some imaginary woman who I've never met before.

GP   That's perfectly normal.

Charles   I fall in love with her.

GP   Absolutely.

Charles   And she loves me . . .

GP   Of course . . .

Charles   Then I lose her.

GP   Everybody has those dreams. Man has dreamt of the elusive perfect partner since time began. It's a very healthy sign for someone in your position. If you were suffering from depression you might not dream at all.

Pause.

Charles   Then this woman turns into a cat.

GP   I see . . .

Charles   Next thing I know I'm rogering the cat. And it's only afterwards that I realise that this is no ordinary cat but . . . it's my cat.
From when I was a little boy. A tom-cat.

Pause.

I felt so guilty.

Silence.

GP   Obviously you're still quite depressed.
And this gives rise to morbid thoughts.
Questions about the past and guilt about trivial things . . .

Charles   Trivial things . . . how trivial?

GP   It could be anything, things which ordinarily wouldn't trouble you at all.

Pause.

Were you happily married?

Charles   We had the occasional ruck. Who doesn't?

GP   Nothing serious?

Charles   She'd always wanted children.

GP   Did you?

Slight pause.

Charles   Even if we could have had a family . . .

GP   'Even if . . . '?

Pause.

Charles   See, I bought the bar when everybody was buying a place. A year later they're all going into middle management – but I stay put. Her body clock is ticking away and she wants kids and pets and a front lawn and a mortgage and holidays in Orlando . . . and I think that she thought I didn't care about that. But I did care. I cared about her with every drop of life in my body. I cared about her and I adored her more than life itself.

Pause.

But I had a business to run.

Pause.

I told her, 'It beats working for some bastard in a Merc.'

Pause.

That's when I started drinking. On the sauce every other night.

GP   I see.

Charles   Piss-arsed legless every night. Stinking. Senseless.

GP   Mm.

Charles   Shitless. Bombed. Maudlin.

GP   Yes.

Charles   Then I stopped. Just in time.

Pause.

GP   You stopped. Altogether?

Charles   She stopped me.

GP   So you no longer drink.

Charles   I have a glass of wine every now and then.

GP   Shall we say a glass a night?

Charles   More or less.

GP   So, that's seven glasses a week.

*The **GP** scribbles calculations.*

Charles   I have the odd bottle, every now and then.

GP   Maybe a beer after work?

Charles   Couple of beers, yeah.

GP   Spirits?

Charles   Bottle a week maybe.

GP   A week?

Charles *adds up on his fingers. He switches hands and adds up more.*

Charles   Sometimes.

GP   That's more than thirty units a week.

Charles   Yeah, scrub the beer.

GP   Mm, twenty's really the limit.

Charles   I'm good at it. I have a 'strong' constitution.

Laughs. Pause.

GP   Perhaps you need a holiday.

Charles   I don't have time for a holiday.

GP   Have an away day. How often do you exercise?

Charles   Never.

GP   You should try to exercise. It really does help to take your mind off things.

Charles   Does it?

GP   You'd be surprised.

Charles   I am surprised.

GP   Or I could arrange some counselling.

Charles   What about drugs?

GP   Drugs?

Slight pause.

Charles   Pills. I mean proper drugs, I mean, I've heard good reports about, you know, drugs.

GP   I'd give you counselling before I gave you medication.

Charles   Which is better?

GP   That's really up to you to decide.

Charles   Which is quicker?

GP   Ah, the blind faith of man in modern medicine.

Charles   Well, what else is there?

GP   Other than counselling?

Charles   Yeah.

GP   That's up to you as well.

Silence.

Charles   This is fucking nonsense.

GP   Sorry?

Charles   This is rubbish. You're paid to help me.
'Have an away day.'
You're a doctor.

He goes.

Scene Five

Club.

Charles *and the* **Maître d'** *sprawl at a table, drinking coffee and smoking cigarettes.*

Charles   Blah blah blah. Blah blah blah. Blah blah blah blah blah.

Pause.

Eh? Innit?

Pause.

Eh? All talk. (*Snorts.*) They're all cunts. 'Have an away day'? (*Snorts.*)

Maître d'   Where?

Charles   Absolutely. 'Where would you recommend, doc?'

Maître d'   No, I'm asking you. Where would you go?

Charles   Well, I wouldn't, would I?

Maître d'   Why not? Take the doctor's advice.

Pause.

Charles   My dream is to have an away day. What I would give to have an away day. I'd go tomorrow if I had someone to go with.

Maître d'   Go by yourself.

Charles   And someone to hold the fort.

Maître d'   Close for the day.

Charles   No. It wouldn't be the same.

Pause.

A waitress, **Lucy***, comes over wearing a short skirt, black stockings, suspenders, white blouse and heels. She is carrying a bottle of wine. She shows the* **Maître d'** *the label, he nods, she pours, he tastes, she pours a full glass and he places his hand on her arse.*

Lucy   Oi. I won't tell you again.

Maître d'   What are you going to do?

She exits.

Maître d'   Bugger off to Malaga for the week.

Charles   Turn it in. Malaga?

Maître d'   What's wrong with Malaga?

Charles   Oh, stop. The Costa?

Maître d'   Malaga's not the Costa.

Charles   It's near the Costa.

Maître d'   Well, where do you want to go?

Charles   Somewhere hot.

Maître d'   Florida.

Charles   Camber Sands.

Maître d'   Don't be a cunt. Nobody goes to Camber Sands.

Charles   I used to go to Camber Sands with the missus. She loved it.

Maître d'   Oh, used to ... certainly. Everybody used to.

Pause.

Charles   You know I can still smell the salt, the odour of salt and sun cream on her skin. Sometimes I smell her perfume. Straight up. I can walk past a bird, a complete stranger, and suddenly bosh. I'm gone. What is that?

Maître d'   Memories.

Charles   Yeah.

Maître d'   I'm so sorry, Charles. If I knew what to say, I'd say it.

Lucy *returns with a bowl of water and puts it on the table. The* **Maître d'** *runs a hand up her leg and she steps back quickly.*

Lucy   Cheeky bugger.

Maître d'   No.

Lucy   That is rude.

Maître d'   Is it?

Lucy   Yeah.

Maître d'   What are you going to do about it?

Lucy   God.

She exits. **Charles** *sniffs the air.*

Charles   Eh?

Maître d'   Oh, stop.

Charles   Eh?

Maître d'   Turn it in.

Charles   Why? I'm single.

Maître d'   Charles, come on. It's undignified.

Lucy *returns wearing a black gown and mortar-board like a public school teacher and carrying a pepper-mill. She puts her foot on the chair and grinds pepper into the bowl. He puts a hand on her knee. He runs his hand up her leg to her crotch. She slaps him and takes her foot off the chair abruptly.*

Maître d'   Ow.

Lucy   That's naughty.

Maître d'   What did you do that for?

Lucy   I should send you to detention.

Maître d'   That hurt.

Lucy   I should –

Maître d'   Use the cane, the cane.

Lucy   Oh yeah. Whoops.

She extracts a cane from her waistline. **Maître d'** *stands and bends over.* **Lucy** *hesitates, then smacks his arse.*

Maître d'   Harder.

She smacks harder.

Lucy   Like that?

Maître d'   Spaghetti.

Lucy   'Please may I have . . .'

Maître d'   'Please may I have my main course now.'

Lucy   Certainly, sir.

She exits. He rubs his cheek, sighs, sits. Pause.

Charles   How long you been in this lark then?

Maître d'   It's the new thing, Charlie.

Charles   Really?

Pause.

How long have we known each other?

Maître d'   Years.

Charles   Well I'm glad you're around. Because I'm telling you, we live in a world of jobsworths. A world of people with no guts. No soul. But I can come here, any time of the day or night and you always listen.

Lucy *returns with a plate heaped with elastic bands.*

Maître d'   What's this?

Lucy   Your spaghetti.

Maître d'   Elastic bands. I said spaghetti.

Lucy   Spaghetti is elastic bands.

Maître d'   Spaghetti is shoe-laces. Elastic bands is green salad. What's dessert?

Lucy   Summer pudding.

Maître d'   No, what represents dessert? What's summer pudding?

Lucy   Sponges?

Maître d'   Sponge scourers.

Lucy   You want me to fetch dessert?

Maître d'   No just . . . put that down.

She puts down the plate.

What are you wearing underneath your gown?

Slight pause.

Lucy   Wouldn't you like to know?

Maître d'   I do know, for Christ's sake. You're wearing your fucking blouse, aren't you? Remove your blouse when you don the gown in future.
Do you want to learn this or not?

Lucy   Yeah.

Maître d'   How many times have we been through this? You've been at it a week and you can't carry out the simplest instructions.

She doesn't respond.

Do you know how many girls would give their eye teeth to work here?

She starts to go.

Take my plate.

As she takes it he grabs her around the waist and puts a hand down her cleavage.

Maître d' (*growls*).

She struggles, he holds tight, she slaps him and breaks away.

Ow! Stop doing that!

Lucy   You're supposed to like it.

Maître d'   Use the cane for fuck's sake!

Lucy   It was only a slap.

He stands clutching his cheek.

Maître d'   Never hit people in the head! OK? You'll knock somebody out.

He sits. She leans over to get the plate, he pinches her bottom, she steps back and pulls out the cane.

Maître d'   OK, fine. Now what do you say?

Lucy   'Would you like to go to detention?'

Maître d'   OK. 'No, thank you.'

He holds out a fifty-pound note. She doesn't take it.

Lucy   What's this?

Maître d' (*sighs*)   It's your 'tip'.

She reaches out to take it and he drops it on the floor, sweeps it under the table with his foot.

Maître d'   Well, do you want it or not?

Lucy   No, thank you very much.

Maître d'   You don't need an extra nifty?

Charles   My God, is that the time?

Lucy   No.

Maître d'   On your wages? Must be joking.

Charles   I best be off, eh?

Maître d'   No, you're all right.

Lucy   I think I'd prefer it behind the bar.

Maître d'   Pick it up.

Charles   Places to go, people to see.

Maître d'   Get under the table and pick it up, you bitch!

Charles   Uh, listen, old son . . .

Maître d'   (*to* **Charles**)   In a minute.

Lucy *gets under the table on hands and knees.* **Charles** *stands and paces, embarrassed. The* **Maître d'** *rolls his eyes, and gestures with his hand.*

And so on and so forth. That's fine. Any questions?

Lucy   I've had enough of this.

She starts to go.

Maître d'   Now what?

Lucy   I'm not that type of woman.

He laughs slightly.

Maître d'   What type are you?
Come on.

Pause.

Lucy   I'm shy.

Maître d'   'Shy?' Men like shy women.

Lucy   I don't know what I'm doing.

Maître d'   Men like women who don't know what they're doing.

Lucy   It's driving me mad.

Maître d'   Men like mad women.

Charles   Mad women are great . . .

Maître d'   The point is, you're not really mad. You're not really shy.

Lucy   I'm not a prostitute.

Maître d'   Hey Hey Hey!

Pause. They all look at each other. **Charles** *goes and waits by the door.*

I can't afford to keep losing people. It makes the clientele jumpy.

Lucy   The clientele are already jumpy.

Maître d'   You belong here. Take a day off and you'll come back refreshed.

Lucy   (*tuts*).

She goes.

Maître d'   Lucy, you come back here.

She reaches the door.

If you walk out that door you'll regret it.

She exits.

If you're not back in twenty-four hours you'll regret it.

Charles *fidgets. Snorts. 'Growls.'*

Silence.

Charles *starts to go.*

Maître d'   Nice to see you again, Charles. Stay in touch.

Charles   We'll have a bevvie.

Maître d'   When I'm not so busy, perhaps.

Charles *exits.*

Scene Six

Bar.

Charles *stands behind the bar.* **Lucy** *sits on a stool on the other side of the bar.*

Lucy   ... So when the clientele misbehaved you had to smack 'em. Thing was, the more you smacked 'em the more they misbehaved, the dirty old sods.

Charles (*snorts*)   Ridiculous.

Lucy   Nah, that was the fun bit.

Charles   How d'you mean?

Lucy   Makes a change to be dishing it out for once. (*Laughs.*)

Charles   How d'you mean?

Lucy   Nothing.

Pause.

I wasn't very good at it.

Pause.

D'you have music?

Charles   No.

Lucy   Why not?

Charles   It's a boozer. People come here to booze.

Lucy   Oh.

Pause.

Charles   What was he paying you?

Lucy   Tenner an hour plus tips.

Charles   More than you'll get here.

Lucy   It's the principle, isn't it?

Charles   Where d'you live?

Lucy   Tooting Bec. Next door to the Lido.

Charles   Classy.

Lucy   Nah, it's just a bedsit.

Charles   It's quite a walk away.

Lucy   I don't mind.

Slight pause.

Charles   You're not a student, are you?

Lucy   Do I look like a student?

Charles   I can't have you pissing off to become a geologist all of a sudden.

Lucy   Nah, been in catering since school, haven't I?

Charles   Get your thingies, did you?

Lucy   How d'you mean?

Charles   Qualifications. A levels.

Lucy   All that. Yeah.

Charles   You've got A levels?

Lucy   Absolutely . . . lots.

Charles   And you wanna work in a pub?

Pause.

Lucy   Actually . . . I packed it in when I was fifteen.

Charles   How come?

Lucy   I was expelled.

Charles   What for?

Lucy   Oh . . . I don't know . . . something trivial.
(*Laughs.*) Stealing. Arson.

Charles   Oh, stop.

Lucy   Alcoholism. Drugs.

Charles   I'll get the giggles.

They laugh.

Pause.

Lucy   No, I was just being difficult, I expect. You know, 'immature'.

Charles   As long as you can pull a pint.

Lucy   Absolutely.

Charles   When can you start?

Lucy   When d'you want me to start?

Charles   Tomorrow.

Lucy   I can start today.

Charles   Tomorrow's better. I've got a bit of business to sort out. I'll show you out.

Lucy   What sort of business?

Charles   It's personal. Don't worry, I'm not going under.

He comes around from behind the bar.

My wife just died. I'm tending the grave today.

Lucy   Oh. I'm sorry.

Charles   No, you're all right.

Lucy   Just making sure.

Charles   It's six quid an hour. You keep your tips, you don't have to spank nobody, no dope fiends, coke-heads, suits or lunatics. D'you want the job or not?

Lucy   'Course.

She joins him at the door.

Charlie   Tomorrow then?

Lucy   Yeah. See you.

She goes.

Charles   Hey.

She comes back.

D'you like rum?

He picks up a bottle from a crate by the door.

Lucy   Not really.

Charles   It's booze, isn't it?

Lucy   I don't drink.

Charles   Why not?

Lucy   I just don't.

Charles   Very wise.

She goes. **Charles** *puts the bottle back.*

Scene Seven

Cemetery.

Charles *places flowers on his wife's grave and stares at it. Nearby a* **Woman** *places flowers on another grave. She sees* **Charles**.

Woman   Hullo. I didn't see you there.

Charles   Hullo. All right?

Woman   Don't I know you?

Charles   Boozer in Garratt Lane.

Woman   I thought you looked familiar.
Who brings you here, if you don't mind me asking?

Charles   My wife. The funeral was on the weekend.

Woman   Oh, shame. Hot or cold?

Charles   How d'you mean?

Woman   Cremated or embalmed?

Charles   Embalmed.

Pause.

Woman   I read where they were supposed to cremate Albert Einstein. Then somebody came along and pinched his brain. Sliced the top of his head clean off like a lid and whipped it out. It's in three pieces now, pickled, somewhere in America.

Charles   Really?

Woman   Yes.

Pause. **Charles** *stares at his wife's grave.*

They took his eyes as well. Yes. Sucked them out with a . . . a sucker and kept them in a jam jar. Like the pope's relics, you know. It's bonkers.

Charles *looks at the* **Woman**

Charles   Bonkers, yeah.

Woman   I'm up the pub after this. Fancy a stiff drink. You're welcome to join me.

Pause.

If you needed some company, that's all I meant.

Pause.

Because you're a very attractive man.

Pause.

It's probably a bit early, I suppose.

Charles   How'd you mean?

Woman   They say it takes three months before you finish mourning properly.

Charles   Three months?

Woman   Well, it all depends on your character, really.

Charles   Character, yeah.

Woman   Your nature.

Charles   Yeah.

Woman   And sometimes it's just not . . . not in your nature. Mind you, if you can bring yourself to be positive about it, the world's your oyster.

Charles   Absolutely.

Pause.

What if you can't?

Woman   Oh, I don't know.

Charles   Dear-oh-dear.

They laugh slightly.

Woman   'Dear-oh-dear', precisely.

She goes.

Scene Eight

Bar.

Closing time. **Charles** *is standing behind the bar, holding a baseball bat and examining it.* **Lucy** *walks in carrying a stack of glasses and whistling. She puts the glasses on the bar.*

Charles   Everybody gone?

Lucy   Yeah.

Charles   That was quick.

Lucy   I've got the touch.

Charles   Cop hold of this.

He hands her the baseball bat.

Lucy   What's this for?

Charles   Guess.

Lucy   I hate to think.

Charles   From time to time people misbehave.

Lucy   I'm not doing any funny stuff.

Charles   You don't have to use it, just look like you know how to.

He brandishes it threateningly.

Lucy   What if it doesn't work?

Charles   Then you have to use it.

Lucy   I wouldn't know where to start.

Charles   I'll show you.

Lucy   Why can't you get a bouncer or something?

Charles   I am the bouncer, love.
And when I'm not here, you're the bouncer.

Lucy   You're making me nervous.

Charles   There's a lot of funny people out there.

He has a few practice swings.

Lucy   You're bloody joking. Anything could happen.

Charles   Like what?

Lucy   I could miss.

Charles   Not if you learn properly. Now, you keep it under
the bar resting in this crate so you can grab it quick. The minute
anybody starts anything you grab it like so . . . and so . . . rest it
on the bar and 'bang'. You slide it across the bar into his guts.
Watch.

He demonstrates the manoeuvre.

Lift . . . and slide. And you want to get him in the solar plexus,
just below the rib cage because you want to wind him, double
him up. Then you come round and you get him on the ground.

He comes around from behind the bar.

Work on his body with clean, crisp smacks. Concentrate on the
pressure points. Backs of the knees, elbows, ankles. Because you
want to immobilise him. Yeah?

Lucy   Yeah . . .

Charles   Surprise him. You have a go.

She goes behind the bar and tries the manoeuvre.

Lucy   Lift . . . and slide. Lift and . . . slide.

Charles   Faster. See, it's all in the wrist. In your technique.

Lucy *practises,* **Charles** *watches.*

Charles   'Cause you want to break his ribs. Get to his vital organs. Teach the fucker a lesson! Go on ... !

Charles *suddenly stares into space.* **Lucy** *stops.*

Lucy   Are you all right?

Charles   What am I saying?

Pause.

What am I like? Eh?

Pause. They look at each other.

Lucy   You look tired.

Charles   It's been a long day.

Pause.

Lucy   You miss her, don't you?

Charles   She was the sweetest, loveliest little girl I ever knew.

Pause.

Not a nasty bone in her body.

Pause.

You know the one thing she loved more than anything else in the world?

Lucy   What's that?

Charles   Her garden.
Clumping about the garden with her little boots on, her hair all over the place, growing things. She was magic with courgettes. She had a gift for courgettes. And her flowers. Not ordinary flowers. Special flowers. Rare, odd, funny coloured things. She had style. Yellow crocus. Jacaranda. Blue irises. Purple irises.

Pause. He puts the bat away.

You hungry?

Lucy   Starved.

Charles   Fancy a Chinese?

Scene Nine

Chinese restaurant.

Charles *and* **Lucy** *raise their glasses, smile and so on.* **Charles**
watches **Lucy** *eat.*

Charles   You remind me of her.

Lucy   Who?

Charles   My wife.

Lucy   I've heard that before.

She stops eating.

Sorry.

Charles   When she was young.

Lucy   Ah.

They eat.

I want to get married one day. I think it must be nice to, you
know, always, you know, have somebody there.

Charles   Absolutely.

Lucy   Somebody to keep you warm at night and all that.

Charles   Yes.

Lucy   Somebody to listen to all your silly ideas. Tell you you
done the right thing when you done the wrong thing. That's
romance, that is. That's what love is.

Pause.

Charles   You don't have a fella then?

Lucy   He's a fucking animal. I mean it. If he walked through
that door right now I'd murder him.

Charles   Ah.

Lucy   Sadistic bastard. I hate him.

Pause.

Actually he's your mate from the club. It was just a fling, really. You must think I'm such a slapper.

Pause.

I know he does.

Charles   I don't.

Lucy   He does.

Charles   I'm sure he doesn't.

Lucy   He does.

Charles *stops eating and pats* **Lucy***'s hand across the table. They look at each other. He takes his hand away.*

Charles   Sorry.

Lucy   I'm not, you know.

Charles   I didn't say you were.

Lucy   Your fucking wife just died.

Charles   I was only . . .

Lucy   What are you like, eh? Mad?

She prods **Charles***'s food with chopsticks, lifts a mouthful to her mouth and eats.*

Lucy   Call this chicken chow mein? Chicken shavings more like. I bet you they've got one chicken chained up out the back and they just shave bits off of it and mix 'em in with a noodle or two, fucking skinflints. Aren't you hungry?

Charles   No.

Lucy   Oh.

She stops eating. Wipes her mouth with a napkin.

Pause.

Charles   I'll get the bill.

Lucy   Bill, bill good idea.

Charles (*to* **Waiter**)   Waiter . . .

Lucy (*to* **Waiter**)   Yoo-hoo, waiter . . .

Silence.

Charles   So. You all right to open up tomorrow?

Lucy   Absolutely.

Charles   Smashing.

Scene Ten

Bar.

The **Maître d'** *lies on the floor in a pool of blood.* **Lucy** *is still clutching the baseball bat in horror.* **Charles** *is squatting down feeling for a pulse.*

Charles   Jesus.

Lucy   Where were you?

Charles   I had things to do.

Lucy   I was waiting for you all day.

Charles   What did you let him in for?

Lucy   He wouldn't go away. He was hammering the door down.

Charles   Fuck.

Charles *goes and locks the door.*

Lucy   Then he started going on about how much he missed me and how sorry he was and how nice I was and how sensible I was. Then he got frisky.

Charles   Frisky?

Lucy   He started threatening me.

Charles   So you let him in?

Lucy   Yeah.

Charles   After he started threatening you?

Lucy   Yeah . . .

Pause.

Charles   You got a mirror?

Lucy   I've got a compact.

Charles   That'll do.

She exits and returns with a handbag from which she extracts the compact.
She gives it to **Charles** *who blows on it and rubs it on his shirt.*

Charles   Covered in shit.

He breathes on it. Taps it.

Covered in powder.

He holds it to the **Maître d'***s mouth.*

Hang about.

He polishes it. Tries again. He hands it back to **Lucy** *and stands.*

Long pause.

Lucy   I was scared.

Charles   I'm scared now. What were you thinking?

Lucy   He had a knife. I panicked.

Charles   What sort of knife?

Lucy   A small one.

Charles   So he attacked you with a knife?

Lucy   He was about to.

Charles   Did he or didn't he?

Lucy   He really lost his temper. He had that look about him. He had that look in his eyes. He was about to snap . . .

Charles (*pause*)   Has he . . . has he done anything like this before?

Lucy   No. It was a complete surprise.

Charles *fetches a cloth and wipes up the blood.*

Lucy   You don't believe me, do you? You think I'm just being neurotic. Well, don't you?

Pause.

It was an accident. I didn't mean to hurt him.

Charles   You hit him in the head.

Lucy   I was trying to stun him.

Charles (*scrubbing*)   What did I tell you about that, Lucy? You weren't listening, were you? I told you precisely what to do, if there's a problem, we went through the whole procedure, but no, you had a better idea.

He goes behind the bar, wipes his hands and finds a bottle of rum. Opens it and drinks.

I leave you alone for five minutes . . .

Lucy   Oh, don't go on about it!

Charles *goes to the phone on the wall and dials.*

Lucy   What are you doing?

Charles   Phoning the police.

She goes to him and they briefly struggle over the phone.

Lucy   They won't believe me.

Charles   This isn't a game.

Lucy   . . . And it was your idea anyway. You told me to do it. I wouldn't do a thing like that in a million years.

Pause. He puts the phone down.

We could say you did it. Because you were depressed.

Pause.

Charles   Why?

Pause.

People will miss him. His family. His friends.

Lucy   He doesn't have any friends. We're his friends.

Charles   People will come looking for him. People . . . in the community.

Lucy   Who?

Silence.

Charles   Well, what are we going to do with him?

Lucy   We could throw him in the river.

Charles   No.

He picks up the phone and dials.

Lucy   We could bury him on Balham Common. It's a bit more appropriate.

Pause.

And, and easier . . .

Charles   Oh, shut up. Just shut up.

Lucy   It's all winos and hookers. Nobody'll find him.

Charles   We're not doing it.

Lucy   Why not?

Charles   Because it's wrong!

Pause.

And we could get caught.

And then I'll go to prison because it's my bar and my baseball bat and I'm the oldest.

Pause.

How far is Balham Common?

Lucy   Ten minutes in the car.

Pause.

Have you got a car?

He just looks at her, still holding the phone.

Scene Eleven

Balham Common.

Evening. **Charles** *and* **Lucy** *lower the corpse, wrapped in a blanket, into the grave.*

Lucy   He was a vicious, pitiless bastard. He deserved it.

Charles   Much as I liked him, he was a pimp.

Lucy   Yeah.

Charles   I'm glad he's dead.

Lucy   Me too.

Charles   If a man can't play by the rules then he deserves every dark fucking day that befalls him.

Pause.

He wants to come into my place, with a knife, start throwing his weight around, he's got no manners, then it's not my problem.

Pause.

The good Lord giveth and He taketh and we, God bless us, made in His image, do the same and so fuck it.

Pause.

It makes me so angry, Lucy.

Lucy   D'you think we should say a prayer or something?

Charles   What sort of prayer?

Lucy   I don't know.

He looks at her, then pulls his Bible out of his coat pocket and flips through it. After a moment, he shuts it and hands it to **Lucy**.

Charles   Go on.

Lucy *looks through the Bible, shuts it and hands it back.* **Charles** *puts it in his pocket, takes out a flask of rum and drinks. He puts the flask away and fills in the grave.* **Lucy** *gazes at the corpse.*

Lucy   He doesn't look dead.

Pause.

Lucy   What if he isn't? I mean, you're not a doctor.

Charles *stops work.*

Lucy   What if I tell someone? You know what I'm like.

Charles *gets back to work. Pause.*

Lucy   I've seen a few dead bodies in my time.

Charles   Really.

Lucy   My aunty died when I was thirteen. I saw her in her casket. She was yellow. And sort of waxy. Her skin looked like wax.

Charles   Sometimes they use wax if there's any wounds.

Lucy   There wasn't any wounds.

Charles   They drain the blood out which is what makes the skin go yellow.

Lucy   She gassed herself. Stuck her head in the oven. It was sad. She was always so cheerful and positive about things.

Pause.

I've known a lot of people who've died suddenly.

Charles   I haven't.

Lucy   Well, you're older. It's different for you.

Charles   Is it?

Lucy   Different generation. People do more now, don't they? Experience more.
Take more risks. Then there's suicides.
Everybody I know knows somebody who's either thought about it or tried it or actually done it.

Charles   Yes, all right.

Lucy   Live life while you can, when you can, as fast you can. Within reason. That's my motto.

He stops work.

Charles   What is the matter with you?

Lucy   D'you think there is something the matter with me?

Charles   Yes.

Lucy   What?

Charles   I don't know.

Charles *works*.

Lucy   Nearly finished?

Charles *flings the shovel down*.

Charlie   Are you thick or something?

Lucy   No.

Charles   Well, what is it?

Lucy   I don't know.

Charles *tramps down the dirt*.

Lucy   I expect this means I'm out of a job.

Pause.

I didn't have to stay you know, I could have fucked off home
hours ago.

Charles   Why didn't you?

Lucy   I don't know. I'd be bored.

Charles   We should open up. It'll look suspicious.

Pause.

Get in the car.

Lucy   Are you sure?

Charles   Get in the car before I change my mind. In the . . . in
the front.

Lucy   How d'you mean?

Charles   In the front where I can keep my eye on you.

Lucy   I'm not a child.

Charles   I know that.

Pause.

Lucy   Why are you doing this?

Charles   Stop asking questions.

Lucy   I want to know why.

Charles   Because I want to.

Lucy   Just tell me why.

Charles *picks up the blanket and folds it carefully.*

Charles   I don't know why.

She goes. He looks at the grave, picks up the shovel and goes.

Blackout.

Act Two

Scene One

Charles's *flat.*

Charles *is sitting on a bed, holding a phone and drinking from a tumbler. A bottle sits nearby.*

Charles   Mum?

Slight pause

Dad, it's me. Charles.

Pause.

I'm all right. Yeah.

Pause.

It was all right. It was nice.

Pause.

Dozens. Yes. She was a popular girl.
Yes, she was lovely. I know that.

Pause.

Very pretty.

Pause.

It was a lovely day, yes.

Pause.

Lovely. Nice and hot.

Slight pause.

Smashing. All week. Beautiful. Listen dad . . . No, don't get
mum just yet. I want to talk to you.

Pause.

I just want to talk. See how you are.

Pause.

Who? Which side?

Pause.

He packs a chiv, I know. He's a cunt.

Slight pause.

His son's a cunt as well.

Slight pause.

They're a pair of cunts. The uncle's a cunt with glasses. Which makes him a glunt, yeah, very funny, Dad . . . I know they drink here but I never make them welcome. No, he's in Parkhurst – oh, really . . . ? Look, apart from that – you're well in yourself, yeah? Cutting down on the fags?

Pause.

And mum? No, don't go and get her. I want to talk to you. I just want to . . . all right put her on.

Pause.

Hullo, Mum. How are you?

Long pause.

I know he is, Mum . . . Friday . . . got a keg of spillage especially for him. Parkhurst. No, the old man was in Wandsworth . . .

Slight pause.

He never hanged himself, you're getting confused . . . that doesn't mean that he did . . . I know you do. I know you do. I wish he did too.

Pause.

The funeral was lovely. Lovely day, yes . . . how are you, you, Mum? Never mind me.

Pause.

Marvellous. That's all I wanted to hear. I have to go now.

Slight pause.

Nothing's wrong. I'm just tired.

Slight pause.

You're absolutely right, Mum. Housework?
No. Can't say that I have been.

Pause.

I don't want a new girlfriend. You're absolutely ... but ... oh,
good plan, Mum.

Pause.

No, I'm just a bit ... 'sad', yeah.

Pause.

No ... no ... no ... something happened in the bar and what
with one thing and another ...

Slight pause.

Three square meals a day, Mum. Spam? You're absolutely
right. Yes, Mum. I have to go now, Mum. Y – all right. Ta ta.
Ta ta. Love to dad. Ta ta.

He hangs up and drinks.

Scene Two

Bar.

A lock-in is in progress. Music plays. **Lucy** *and fellow* **Drinkers** *sing
along drunkenly.* **Charles** *wipes the bar and clears up.*

Drinkers   When no one else can understand me
When everything I do is wrong
You give me hope and consolation
You give me strength to carry on

Lucy *(simultaneously)*   Join in, Charlie.

He doesn't.

Drinkers   And you're always there to lend a hand
In everything I do

> That's the wonder, the wonder of you
> Da de da, da de da, da de da . . .

Charles *turns the music off. He opens a bottle of rum and drinks from the bottle.*

Silence.

Drinker One   Lord Almighty, I feel my temperature rising . . .

Pause.

Drinker Two   Moody blue, what am I coming to . . .

Drinker One   I'm just a hunka hunka burning love . . .

Woman   Charlie Charlie Charlie Charlie Charlie . . . This man . . . is a . . . where did my glass go?

Drinker One   Hello, cheeky chops . . .

Lucy   I don't remember your name.

Drinker Two   I planted my wife a week after my fortieth birthday. I stood around the grave with the in-laws discussing the weather . . .

Drinker One   Forgotten already?

Woman   Leave her alone, she's only little.

Drinker Two   Her mother had a smile like a thin streak of piss . . .

Drinker One   I think you are a dangerous woman.

Drinker Two   The old man had regressed into a sort of childlike hysteria somewhere around the third day of his honeymoon and hadn't spoken since . . .

Woman   Ignore him, pet, he's been in Parkhurst the past five years . . .

Lucy   No! What did you do?

Silence.

Sorry.

Pause.

I wasn't being funny.

Drinker One *laughs suddenly.*

Drinker One   What a character!

Lucy   I wasn't saying anything or anything . . .

Drinker One   Isn't she a character, Charles?

Woman   You leave her alone, you big hairy bastard, she don't know.

Drinker Two   The heavens pissed buckets and I stared into the hole and reflected on the banality that had gone before . . .

Lucy   I was just interested.

Drinker One   Never ask me that again.

Lucy   I won't.

Drinker Two   . . . . And the banality that was to come.

Drinker One   Have I met you before? You remind me of someone.

Pause.

Lucy   I've heard that before.

Woman   Don't take any notice of him, love, he's a pervert.

Drinker One   Listen to me, no listen – you are a devastatingly handsome young woman. Devastatingly . . .

Lucy   Oh, stop . . .

Woman   Should pick on somebody his own age . . .

Lucy   'A devastatingly handsome young . . . '?

Woman   Live your life, girl, that's what you should do.

Lucy   He's asking for it, isn't he? Eh?

Charles   Lucy . . .

Lucy   Come on, then. Let's have you.

Charles   Please . . .

Drinker Two   'I'm a Captain of fucking Industry,' I thought. 'But I still shit in a toilet and like everybody else I'm going to die.'

Drinker One   I'm not being funny, I'm attracted to you.

Drinker Two   And the funeral bells tolled and a Mockingbird sang as if to . . .

Lucy   I'll bury you.

Drinker One (*laughing*)   Priceless!

Woman   Don't say that, girl, it's bad luck!

Lucy   I killed somebody, I did.

Woman   Don't say that, girl, someone might believe you!

Lucy   Charles dug a hole and buried the body for me.

Drinker (*laughing*)   Oh, my sainted aunty.

Drinker Two   'I looked, and behold a pale horse and his name that sat on him was Death, and Hell followed with him . . .'

Woman   No, you are joking!

Lucy   Yes – no!

Drinker Two   Which is to say, 'The shit is really going to hit the fan now.'

Lucy   He died right there, right where you're all standing.

Drinker One   Is this true, Charlie? Little girl says you and her stiffed a geezer.

Silence.

Woman   Not the wife, you mean?

Lucy   No, somebody else.

Drinker One   Oh, stop! I'll have a bloody heart attack in a minute.

Pause.

Woman   You're pulling our legs.

Lucy   It's true.

Drinker Two   This is unbelievable.

Woman   How did you kill him?

Drinker One   This is my type of lady.

Lucy   I hit him.

Drinker One   Chinned him? That's the stuff.

Lucy   I beat the shit out of him.

Drinker Two   Outrageous.

Woman   What, a drunk?

Lucy   Actually . . .

Drinker One   'Actually, *actually*.' Go on.

Pause.

Lucy   You won't believe me.

Drinker One   You're all right . . . say it.

Lucy   No.

Drinker One   Say it.

Woman   What, what say what?

Lucy   Don't laugh.

Slight pause.

He was my lover.

Woman   No . . .

Lucy   Yes.

Woman   Fuck off . . .

Lucy   Fucking done him in him because . . .

Woman   Is this true, Charlie?

Drinker One   Classic . . .

Lucy   Because he was hurting me . . .

Drinker One (*laughing*)   Absolutely.

Drinker Two   And you got away with it?

Lucy   It's not funny.

Drinker One   This is hysterical!

Lucy   Tell 'em, Charlie. Charles . . .

Charles *stares into space.*

Pause.

Lucy   Are you going to vomit?

Woman   Get a bucket, someone . . .

Lucy   Charles, what's wrong?

Woman   Quick, Charlie's gonna vomit.

*The **Woman** goes behind the bar and comes back with a bucket. She waits with the bucket.*

Lucy   I feel awful.

Charles (*to **Lucy***)   You're drunk.

Drinker One   Aha! I thought so. I could tell.

Woman   What did he say? What was that?

Charles   Don't fuck about.

Lucy   The poor man.

Charles   Don't say another word.

Woman   Did she or didn't she?

Lucy   I am such a bitch.

Charles   Do you hear me? Do You Understand?

Woman   I won't tell anyone, I promise. Come on, Charlie . . . Charles . . . ?

Pause.

Charles   Believe what you want to believe.

Pause.

Woman   What are you like, eh? Did he try and touch you up?

Drinker Two   I do not believe this. She admits to slaughtering a living person on this exact spot . . .

Drinker One   Watch it . . .

Drinker Two   What was his name?

Woman   Oh, you can't ask that . . .

Drinker Two   No, we have a right to know . . .

Drinker One   Oh, do we? How jolly.

Charles   HEY! SHUT UP!

Pause.

Who are you people? What do you know about anything? You come here every night and drink and piss and moan and laugh and line up like so many pigs at a fucking trough. You're ignorant.

Silence.

Woman   You've upset him now.

Charles   What's it like to be so fancy-free, eh? Nothing whatsoever occupying your minds. Come on, I'm interested.

A long pause. **Lucy** *goes to* **Charles**.

Woman   So. How long have you two known each other?

Charles   Get out. Go on. Piss off, the lot of you.

Pause.

Charles *stands and 'fronts'* **Drinker One**. *Pause.*

Drinker One   Don't do anything you'll regret, Charlie-boy.

Pause. The **Drinkers** *slowly file out.* **Charles** *sits.* **Lucy** *sits too and holds his hand.*

Lucy   Shh. It's all right. I'll look after you.

Scene Three

Seaside.

Lucy *and* **Charles** *sit in deck-chairs side by side on the sea front. The sound of gulls overhead.*

Lucy   Cup of tea?

Charles   Lovely.

She pours a cup from a flask and hands it to him. Pours her own cup and they sip.

Lucy   Digestive?

Charles   Ta.

She hands him a biscuit.

Lucy   Holiday.

Charles   Lovely. Thank you.

Lucy   It's a pleasure.

Charles   Yeah.

Pause.

My old man says if you've got one friend in this life you're a lucky man. One person who you can still trust, when you're eighty years old, then you're a lucky man.

Pause.

You know, the one person he listens to? And the one person who listens to him? My dear old mum.

Lucy   Bless 'em.

Charles   Bless 'em. 'As long as you have your health,' she'd say, 'as long as you're still alive and still half-sane, what more can you expect? Eh? Keep things simple. Because the human race, son, is not worth a flying fucking bag of nuts.'

Pause.

Lucy   My parents divorced when I was ten. Spent most of the time 'round my aunty's.

Charles   Oh, I'm sorry.

Lucy   I never liked them. Too quiet.

Charles   Yeah.

Lucy   Not very affectionate.

Charles   No.

Lucy   Not much fun at all really.

Pause.

Still, I don't suppose parents are meant to be fun, are they?

Slight pause.

They're meant to be dignified.

Pause.
They link arms.
They look at each other.
They kiss.

Charles   Bloody hell.

Lucy   Whoops.

Charles   Sorry –

Lucy   No –

Charles   I –

Lucy   I –

Charles   You . . .

Pause.

Lucy   Isn't it a lovely . . . windy day?

Charles   Lovely.

Pause.

Lucy   You must think I'm such a slapper.

Charles   Don't say that.

Lucy   I'm not.

Charles   Why do you say these things?

Lucy   I don't know.

Charles   No, why? I really want to know.

Long pause.

Lucy   They say people do this after a trauma.

Pause.

You become closer to people. Out of relief. It's like you realise how lucky you are.

Charles   It was ... it was inevitable.

Scene Four

Hotel.

Charles *is lying in bed.* **Lucy** *comes into the room wearing only knickers and bra. She has a towel around her head. She takes the towel off her head and shakes her wet hair loose. Sits on the end of the bed and brushes her hair. She applies talcum powder to her body.* **Charles** *watches.*

Charles   You know what I'm turning into? An unprincipled man.

Pause.

I find it easier to take a long hard look at myself after a good shag.

Lucy (*tuts*)   You're in a jolly mood all of a sudden.

Charles   I was just thinking how lovely it is to watch a woman dress. I'm not being funny. I used to watch my wife getting dressed in the mornings. Doing her hair, rubbing in the talcum powder. Makes being alive worthwhile.

Pause.

She was extremely clean. Always filling the bathroom with special little soaps and all sorts of new scents and smells. Always grooming herself. I got quite a kick out of watching her shave her legs. Legs, armpits, marvellous.

Lucy *puts on a sweater.*

Lucy   Really?

Charles   Yes.

Lucy *picks up a skirt and goes to the window. She opens the curtains and window and stands looking out, holding the skirt.*

Charles   I remember our honeymoon. I remember her sitting on the bed in the hotel, with the sun and the sea-air streaming in and her skin and her wet hair all golden in the light, gulls cawing in the distance, and I thought to myself, What does this mean? Eh? This is the only thing that matters.
Fuck work. I'm a cunt.

Pause.

We were in love. Love's great. Love wears a white hat.

Lucy   Are you going to get up or are you going to just stare at my arse all morning?

Charles   Come here, babe.

Lucy   Oh, stop. You're not going to get all soppy on me, are you?

Charles   I already have, girl.

Lucy   Because you know that was just a fuck, don't you?

Slight pause.

Charles   How d'you mean?

Lucy   A quick fuck to keep our spirits up.

Charles   It worked.

Lucy   It doesn't mean anything.

Charles   Really?

Lucy   Because you know this is what ruins friendships, isn't it?

Charles   I know.

Lucy   And we don't want that to happen, do we?

Charles   No ... of course.

Lucy   I don't want anybody getting the wrong end of the stick.

Charles   Who?

Lucy   You. I couldn't cope with another fiasco.

Pause.

Charles   Well, they certainly broke the mould when they made you.

Pause.

I nev . . . I never know whether to laugh or cry.

She goes to him.

Lucy   Look at you.
Big fat belly, hairy arse, toe-nails need cutting, you stink, boozer's breath, hungover again, big hairy bollocks like a gorilla, big ugly cock, look at it, look at all those veins. You haven't got a pot to piss in, no future, you're moody, ugly, bad tempered, old . . .

She kisses him.

What do you want for breakfast?

She puts her skirt on.

Charles   Toast?

Lucy *picks up the phone by the bed, dials, and clears her throat.*

Lucy   Toast for room nine.

She hangs up.

Scene Five

Bar.

Lucy *is working behind the bar.* **Drinker One** *is sitting at the bar with a drink, drunk.*

Drinker   Drink?

Pause.

I'm having one. You're not busy.

Lucy   You're drunk.

Drinker   Eh?

Lucy   No more drinks.

Drinker   Eh?

Lucy   You're drunk. No more.

Drinker   What is it? Rum and Coke?

Lucy   I won't tell you again.

Drinker   Just a tipple.

Lucy   (*tuts*).

Drinker   You know what I like about this stuff? When you drink, the world's still out there, it just doesn't have you by the balls.

Lucy   Oh, absolutely.

Pause.

Drinker   I always wanted to own a fancy wine emporium. A fancy one in the Fulham Road perhaps, or New Malden. As a matter of fact, I was once mooted for a job with Balls Brothers. Only they said I was an alcoholic. Wound up running the Cash 'n' Carry in Wandsworth. Briefly. Before my incarceration.

Lucy   Really?

Drinker   Mm.

Lucy   I *say*.

She yawns. Pause.

Drinker   You know what I like about you? You're always here. I like that. Makes you feel that there are things that are at least a little constant in this world, you know what I'm saying?

Lucy   I would be, wouldn't I?

Drinker   Of course.

Lucy   I'm the barmaid.

Drinker   True.

Lucy   It's my job.

Drinker *nods and stares into his drink.*

Pause.

Drinker   Sad about the guvnor's wife.

Pause.

Well, he wasn't to know, was he?

Pause.

That's what married life is about. The good times and the bad. So long as you have your health and you don't hate each other's guts by the end then you're on top, in my book.

Lucy   What you on about?

Drinker (*tuts*)   The things they used to say about each other. My goodness. Always squabbling and carrying on like a pair of kids. Always rucking, like Tom and Jerry they was. I saw them in Northcote Road market one day, strolling about, hand in hand, bold as brass, and her with a pair of black eyes like a fucking racoon.

Pause.

That's what she was like, see. Spirited. Very emotionally strong and very lively before the separation . . .

Lucy   I beg your pardon?

Drinker   I was just saying . . .

Lucy   I think you've said enough.

Drinker   Funny bloke, Charles. He's a lovely man. One of the best. But you know the only trouble is he's a nutter. Still, I can see why he's drawn to you.

Lucy   Why?

Drinker   F.U.N.

Pause.

Fun.

Lucy Oh, go away.

Drinker Just look at this place. It's on its last legs. It looks . . . clapped. Enjoyed . . . Enjoyed by the men of Wandsworth. Is it still a going concern? Is it still a . . . sound business proposition, do you think? I'll tell you what; this place needs you.

Pause.

As a matter of fact, I get the feeling that if I was to proposition you right now, not in a grubby way, but in a genuine way, you'd say, 'Yes'.

Lucy Sod off!

Drinker Do me a favour. You're gagging for it.

She throws her drink in his face.

Lucy Who do you think you are?

Drinker You'd love it if I took your knickers down and stuck it right up you.

She smacks him in the face. He grabs her wrist and produces a knife. She slips the bat from under the bar and there's a stand-off.

Come on. Have a pop.

Scene Six

Bar.

Charles *enters carrying boxes of alcohol.* **Lucy** *is behind the bar, staring into space.*

Charles Gordon's and Smirnoff thirteen to the dozen. Cunt only tried to stitch me up with more rum. Says he's got a case of Lamb's Navy written in his book. 'And I've got *cunt* written here,' I said. Lamb's Navy? What am I, a fucking sailor? I got him in the corner and I got hold of him and I said, 'Right, you cunt, right . . . Because you people do not give me the respect that I am due. Right,' I said. 'Fuck this, I'll take my business elsewhere. Fuck that,' I said. 'Because I won't take that from no one no more. Lack of respect.'

Pause.

I should have given him a slap.

Pause.

And you know me, Lucy. I'm not a violent man. What's up?

He goes through a door behind the bar to put the boxes down. He comes out.

What happened?

Lucy   He, he had a knife.

Charles   You did it again, I don't believe it.

Lucy   It happened again.

Charles   It's ridiculous!

Lucy   He attacked me.

Charles   Are you mad? My God!

Lucy *goes to him, he backs away.*

Charles   You stay away from me.

Lucy   He said I was a tart.

Charles   Well, are you?

Lucy   Don't you dare say that, what has got into you?

Charles   I'll go berserk in a minute.

Lucy   No wonder your marriage went for a Burton.

Pause.

Charles   What?

Lucy   Nothing.

Charles   What did you say?

Lucy   I'm sorry.

Charles   Who told you this?

Lucy   He did.

The **Drinker** *emerges from the back room looking stunned.*

Charles   And you believed him? Well, do you?

Lucy   No.

Charles   Well, why'd you say it?

Lucy   I don't know.

Charles   After everything I told you.

Pause.

He's a fucking boozer. Why do you talk to these people?

Lucy   He wouldn't go.

Charles   I'll make him go.

The **Drinker** *heads for the door.* **Charles** *follows and grabs his arm.*

Charles   Right, you cunt.

Lucy   Charles, don't.

Charles (*to* **Drinker**)   What have you been saying? Eh?
What did you say about me? Come on.

Drinker   What are you gonna do? Give me a slap?

Lucy   It's a wind-up. He's just trying to get a reaction.

Drinker   She told me all about you.

Charles   You should watch your fucking mouth.

Drinker   Came to me one night with such a face on her . . .

Lucy   I'm not listening.

Charles (to **Lucy**)   No, you're all right, it's all right . . .

Charles *takes out his hankie, hands it to* **Lucy**, *who sniffles and blows
her nose, then without looking, he turns to the* **Drinker** *and beats him to
the floor, punching him repeatedly.*

Lucy   Stop!

Charles   You've got a reaction now!
You've got a reaction now! You've got a reaction now! Eh?
Slag!

Lucy   You'll kill him!

Charles   Shut up!

He raises his hand to slap **Lucy**.

Lucy   No!

Charles   Get out.

Lucy   Don't you dare.

Charles   I mean it.

Lucy   I know you do, Charles.

Pause. He backs off.

Charles   It's none of your business.

Pause.

Don't look at me.

Pause.

What are you looking at?

He goes behind the bar, gets the bat. He smashes up the bar.

This? This?!

Charles *puts the bat down. Goes to the* **Drinker**   *Kneels beside him
and mops blood from the* **Drinker**'s *head with his shirt.*

He'll wake up in a minute. He's just drunk.
Have you got a fag?

Lucy *fetches her bag from behind the bar, rummages in it and hands him a
cigarette.*

Charles   Thank you.

He puts it in his mouth and she lights it.

Thank you.

Lucy puts a cigarette in her own mouth and light it. The **Drinker** *comes to and groans vaguely.*

Lucy   I never did anything, you know. Just kept them company really. Everybody's entitled to that. I don't know how I got into this mess.

Pause.

Charles   I ask myself sometimes did she step in front of the bus on purpose?

Pause.

And I tell myself that's ridiculous. I loved her. I married her.

Lucy   I couldn't do it.

Charles   I haven't got the guts.

Lucy   I've considered it.

Charles   I have too.

Lucy   Tried to think of the best way and so on.

Charles   Me too.

The **Drinker** *eyes them warily and gets up.*

Lucy   I always think of the people I'd leave behind.

Charles   Me too. That's the only thing that worries me.

Drinker   You ... you people are mad.

Charles *pulls out his wallet and offers the* **Drinker** *fifty pounds.*

Charles   Go on. You're all right.

Pause.

I'm apologising.

Pause.

You don't need an extra nifty?

He adds another fifty.

A monkey?

*The **Drinker** takes the money, screws it up and tosses it in **Charles**'s face and exits.*

Charles (*snorts*)   Now I'm bribing people.

Scene Seven

Charles's flat.

Lucy *and* **Charles** *sit on the bed.* **Charles** *drinks from a bottle of vodka and smokes.*

Lucy   Have you ever thought about seeing a shrink?

Pause.

I mean, you were provoked, but you've been under a lot of strain. What if there's something wrong with you? I'm not saying he will press charges, but if he did . . .

Charles   'If, if, if . . . '

Lucy   Who knows what they'll find out?

Charles   If my aunty had balls she'd be my uncle.

Lucy   He'll tell them everything.

Pause.

Charles   We could go abroad. Get away from England.

Lucy   Go abroad?

Charles   Hide.

Lucy   Hide?

Charles   It's a terrible country.

Lucy   With you?

Charles   Nobody works, nobody smiles.

Lucy   I'm going home. I'm going home to watch telly and clean the cooker and do what normal people do.

Charles   I mean, I've got a conscience but I'm not going to torture myself for ever.

He picks up the Bible from by the bed, flips through it.

'The fruit of the Spirit is love, joy, peace, longsuffering, gentleness, goodness, faith, meekness and temperance.' Says who? Eh? Maybe it's not in our nature.

Pause. He drops the Bible.

Lucy   Do you believe in Heaven and Hell?

Charles   I don't know.

Lucy   I used to believe in Heaven.

Charles   I believe in Hell.

Lucy   Obviously there's a Hell.

Charles   I don't know. I don't care.

Lucy   Me neither.

Charles   Not any more.

Pause.

Lucy   I was watching telly, right, and they interviewed a man who said the anti-Christ had come and he knew who it was. He said the anti-Christ is living in south London with a woman half his age. Supposing that's true.

Pause.

Charles (*snorts*)   'The anti-Christ . . . '

Lucy   Don't laugh. I saw it on the telly.

Charles *laughs.*

Stop laughing. It makes sense to me.

Silence.

Charles *drinks.*

Charles   When my wife died, everything went with it. I didn't see the point in being good. I couldn't stop boozing, pay the bills, go to work, come home. Day after day we wade through shit.

Lucy   Oh, stop.

Charles   We grow old waiting for the big reward, something bigger than a good-night kiss, a slap on the back, a sun-tan ...

Lucy   Now you're being silly.

Charles   The Easter Bunny, birthdays, anniversaries, 'Merry Christmas, Charles ... Merry Christmas, everybody ...' I'd rather murder myself.

Lucy   That's enough of that.

Charles   She knew that this life isn't worth living. She never complained, she could always find the good in things, but deep down she knew.

Lucy   Pull yourself together.

Charles   Everybody knows, we're just taught not to think it.

Lucy   You're scaring me.

Charles   We've had it. We're doomed.

Lucy *snatches the bottle and slaps him.*

Lucy   Snap out of it, for God's sake. Do you have to go on and on and on about it? It's so selfish.

Charles   All right ...

Lucy   It's not all right, you ... you ... you monster ... what've ... what have you done ... ?

Pause.

Lucy *puts the bottle down and goes to the door.* **Charles** *follows.*

Charles   Where are you going?

Lucy   Home.

Charles   I'll come with you.

Lucy   Don't be daft.

Pause.

She moves to go and suddenly he grabs her and wrestles her onto the bed.

Lucy   Get off me! What are you doing, you idiot!

After a struggle he gets her shoes off. Holds them up. They look at each other. **Lucy** *pulls out the* **Drinker**'s *knife. They stand.*

Charles   Come on then. Do it. Kill me.

Lucy   I will.

Charles   I know you will. I want to die.

Charles *reaches out for the point of the knife and puts it to his neck.*

Charles   Make sure you get an artery. (*Snorts.*)

Lucy   Don't laugh at me.

Charles   I'm not.

Lucy   I'm not stupid.

Charles   I know.

Lucy   You don't. You think I'm just another scatty woman. It's so typical. I know you think I'm strange.

Charles   I don't.

Lucy   Yes, you do.

Charles   No, I don't.

Lucy   You do.

Charles   I don't.

Lucy   People have always thought that. Even at school. 'Strange.' 'Quirky.' 'Loose.' I'm not. I'm perfectly normal. I'm just different, that's all.

Charles *tries to guide the knife away but she holds it firm.*

Charles   I understand . . .

Lucy   Don't you dare say that. How could you understand? I hate it when people say that. People look straight through me. Like I'm invisible or a . . . a ghost or something. It drives me up the wall.

Charles *takes a step backwards and* **Lucy** *follows.*

Lucy   I'm surrounded by Evil.

Charles   Lucy, babe, listen . . .

Lucy   I am not your 'babe'.

Pause.

She leaves him and paces and fidgets. **Charles** *retrieves the bottle and drinks.*

Charles   I don't want you to leave because the last woman to leave me was dead within weeks.

Lucy   That's different. I don't love you.

Charles   Neither did she.

Lucy   But I like you. And . . . and . . .

Silence.

Lucy *drops the knife, takes the bottle from him and tips it out, drops the empty bottle and falls into his arms. They press their foreheads together and stay like that for a while.*

Charles   Shh. it's all right.

Lucy   I'm scared.

Charles   What are you scared of?

Lucy   Everything.

Charles   Come on. I'll take you home.

Lucy   What colour are ghosts?

Charles   I don't know.

Lucy   Blue?

Charles   Shh.

Scene Eight

Church.

Charles, *wearing an old coat, sits with the* **Vicar**.

Charles   It's like there's this force controlling me or watching over me and making things happen. The things I'm afraid of, and the things I most want, they all happen but I don't ... I don't know why they happen. And, and why me anyway?

Vicar   'O Lord, thou has searched me, and known me. Thou knowest my downsitting, and mine uprising, thou understandest my thoughts from afar.'

Charles   I don't believe in God.

Vicar   Why not?

Charles   Because he doesn't understand, does he? If he did, none of this would have happened.

Pause.

Vicar   Do you believe in destiny?

Charles   I don't know what that means.

Vicar   Many people believe that events are controlled by fate which is predestined by God.

Charles   Or the Devil?

Vicar   Well, no.

Charles   Well, what are you saying?

Vicar   I'm saying perhaps it's the reason you've come to me.

Charles   I came to you because I wanted to.

Vicar   All right ...

Charles   I chose to, understand?

Vicar   Yes, yes I see.

Pause.

Charles   What about my wife? Why did that happen?

Vicar   God has called her to the kingdom of Heaven.

Charles   I know. Why?

Vicar   I don't know why.

Charles   Because it's, it's 'nice' there?

Vicar   These questions can only be answered with faith.

Charles   I don't have any faith.

Vicar   In anything?

Charles   No.

Vicar   You have no faith in humanity?

Charles   No.

Vicar   Faith in love and justice and restitution which has been with us since the birth of civilisation.

Charles   I have faith in love, yeah.

Vicar   Now we're getting somewhere.

Charles   But I don't have anyone to love.

Pause.

Vicar   Perhaps you are ready to be filled.

Charles   Filled?

Vicar   With God's love.

Charles   I don't want God's love. God's love's no good to me. Don't you understand? I've hurt people. I've done things I can't undo.

Vicar   We all hurt people.

Charles   No, I mean, really hurt people . . .

Vicar   And do you think that makes you unworthy of God's love?

Charles   Unworthy?

Vicar   Do you think that makes you unworthy of providence?

Pause.

Charles   I want to confess.

Vicar   To what?

Charles   Do it properly. 'Repent and ye shall be forgiven . . . '

Vicar   It's not that easy.

Charles   Why not?

Vicar   We do not believe in easy redemption. Your restitution is in your hands. You have to do it yourself.

Charles   I've tried doing it myself. It didn't work.

Vicar   Then I say, 'Bring forth fruits worthy of repentance.'

Charles   Listen to me . . .

Vicar   'Bring forth fruits *worthy* of repentance . . . '

Charles   Look at me . . .

Vicar   And talk to God . . .

Charles *grabs the* **Vicar** *roughly.*

Charles   I don't want to talk to God, I want to talk to you! I killed a man. I killed him and I buried him. I beat my wife. I'm bad! All my life I've been bad! 'The brethren you deserve are manifest,' you said. What do I deserve? Eh . . . ?

He lets the **Vicar** *go.*

I'm lost. Don't you understand? I don't know who I am.

Pause.

Vicar   Do the police know about this?

Charles *shakes his head and the* **Vicar** *goes.*

Scene Nine

Cemetery.

Charles, *drunk, stares at his wife's grave.*

Charles   Remember the time I tried to leave? We had a ruck in the middle of the night and I got up and got dressed but you'd hidden my shoes . . . to stop me leaving. But I went anyway . . . in my socks. And you followed me . . . in your dressing-gown . . . and I was walking up Trinity Road and I turned around and you were all hurt and miserable and crying . . . tears streaming down your face . . . little bubbles coming out your nose . . . And you were saying, 'I just want you to come home. I just want you to come home. Don't you understand?'

Pause.

And, and I did understand.

Pause.

I just didn't know why.

Pause.

And then, despite myself, I held out my arms and you snuggled into my arms . . . and suddenly I felt warm . . . I felt part of the world again . . . it seemed like I was doing the right thing for once.

Pause.

And maybe it was the wrong thing. And I'm sorry.

After a moment, a **Police Constable** *and a* **Woman Police Constable** *come over.* **Charles** *stands and stares at the* **WPC**.

PC   Good evening, sir.

Charles   All right?

PC   Would you like to show me some identification?

Charles   Officer, you look just like my wife.

PC   Are you going to show me some identification?

Charles   It's uncanny.

PC   Would you come with us please, sir.

Charles   This is her grave. She's dead. Completely dead.

The **WPC** *takes the bottle. The* **PC** *takes* **Charles**'s *arm.*

WPC Would you like to go to the hospital? Is that where you're meant to be?

Charles No. I've had a few drinks, that's all. I'll be all right in a minute . . .

He tries to walk away. They take hold of **Charles** *and pin his arms behind. He struggles.*

What are you doing?

PC Are you going to co-operate?

Charles I have a right to be here.

WPC Yes, come along, don't make a fuss now.

Charles I'm praying.

PC I'm arresting you for threatening behaviour and drunk and disorderly conduct, understand?

Charles I'm in mourning, the vicar knows I'm here . . . I touched his cassock, that's all, I grabbed hold of his cassock.

They pull his coat down around his arms, revealing his bloodstained shirt.

Charles Hey, I'm not a dosser . . .

PC What's all this?

Charles What?

PC This blood.

Pause.

Charles *takes out ID, gives it to the* **WPC** *who studies it and hands it to the* **PC** *who also studies it.*

Charles Look, my name is Charles Strong. I own the White Horse on Garratt Lane. I've been working all night . . .

PC Charles Strong, I'm arresting you for assault.

Charles No, I was drunk . . . I had an accident . . .

PC Why were you drunk?

Charles I was a bit mixed up. Business is bad . . . one thing leads to . . .

PC   So you decided to attack somebody.

Charles   No.

PC   Did this person attack you?

Charles   No. But . . . earlier . . .

PC   Well, why did you attack him? Eh? You could have killed him.

Charles   My wife, you see . . .

PC   He attacked your wife, did he?

Charles   No, obviously . . .

PC   Obviously . . . is it obvious?

Charles   Listen to me, help me, please . . . My wife was hit by a bus . . . I had a few problems . . . I was . . . I was . . . I was . . . I was lonely . . .

Pause.

And now all this . . . Eh?

Pause.

PC   Are you finished?

Charles   It's difficult to explain.

WPC   Come along then. We'll have a nice cup of tea and you can tell us all about it.

Charles   You're just like her. I mean it. I think you're lovely. Isn't she lovely?

They lead him away.

Blackout.